EGYPT

BY AMY RECHNER

BELLWETHER MEDIA • MINNEAPOLIS, MN

Blastoff! Discovery launches a new mission: reading to learn. Filled with facts and features, each book offers you an exciting new world to explore!

This edition first published in 2019 by Bellwether Media, Inc.

No part of this publication may be reproduced in whole or in part without written permission of the publisher.
For information regarding permission, write to Bellwether Media, Inc., Attention: Permissions Department,
6012 Blue Circle Drive, Minnetonka, MN 55343.

Library of Congress Cataloging-in-Publication Data

Names: Rechner, Amy, author.
Title: Egypt / by Amy Rechner.
Description: Minneapolis, MN : Bellwether Media, Inc., 2019. |
    Series: Blastoff! Discovery: Country Profiles | Includes
    bibliographical references and index. |
    Audience: Ages 7-13.
Identifiers: LCCN 2018000618 (print) | LCCN 2018001791
    (ebook) | ISBN 9781626178427 (hardcover : alk.
    paper) | ISBN 9781681035833 (ebook)
Subjects: LCSH: Egypt–Juvenile literature.
Classification: LCC DT49 (ebook) | LCC DT49 .R43 2019
    (print) | DDC 962–dc23
LC record available at https://lccn.loc.gov/2018000618

Editor: Rebecca Sabelko   Designer: Brittany McIntosh

Printed in the United States of America, North Mankato, MN.

TABLE OF CONTENTS

A MYSTERIOUS WONDER

THE GREAT SPHINX AND
PYRAMIDS OF GIZA

AN UNEXPECTED FIND

In 2017, scientists discovered a previously unknown empty space inside the Great Pyramid. It is believed to be part of the design, but no one knows why the space is there.

The outline of the pyramids towers in the distant morning sky. A family gets in a cab and makes their way to Giza. The giant shapes grow in size as they get closer and closer. Finally, the Great Sphinx comes into view. Its head of a **pharaoh** and body of a lion sit waiting. The family marvels upon the mystery of this creation.

They spend the rest of the afternoon exploring the pyramids before returning to Cairo. They hear the Muslim call to prayer as they arrive at their hotel. Ancient wonders and modern comforts collide in Egypt!

Egypt is in the northeast corner of Africa. It covers 386,662 square miles (1,001,450 square kilometers). The waves of the Mediterranean Sea wash upon Egypt's northern shores. The African countries of Libya and Sudan make up its western and southern borders. Cairo, Egypt's capital, rests in the north.

The northeastern part of Egypt is called the Sinai **Peninsula**. It shares a border with Israel and an **Arab** territory called the Gaza Strip. Just west of the peninsula is the 120-mile (193-kilometer) long Suez **Canal**. This waterway connects the Mediterranean Sea to the **Gulf** of Suez. The gulf flows into the Red Sea, which covers the rest of Egypt's eastern border.

LIBYA

MEDITERRANEAN
SEA

GAZA
STRIP

PORT SAID

ISRAEL

ALEXANDRIA

CAIRO

SUEZ
CANAL

SINAI
PENINSULA

SAUDI
ARABIA

GULF OF
SUEZ

NILE
RIVER

EGYPT

LUXOR

RED SEA

SUDAN

A COUNTRY ON TWO CONTINENTS

Although Egypt is in Africa, its Sinai Peninsula is on the
Asian continent. According to mapmakers, Israel, Jordan,
and the Sinai Peninsula are part of Southwest Asia.

7

LANDSCAPE AND CLIMATE

Egypt's landscape is mostly dry and **arid**. Western Egypt is covered by the Sahara Desert. The Eastern Desert lies along the eastern coast. Dry, rocky land gives way to mountains at the Sinai Peninsula's southern tip. Sometimes an **oasis** will interrupt the endless desert landscape. Egypt's main inland water comes from the Nile, the world's longest river. It flows north to the Mediterranean Sea.

= SAHARA DESERT

MT. SINAI

N
W—E
S

DAKHLA OASIS
WESTERN DESERT

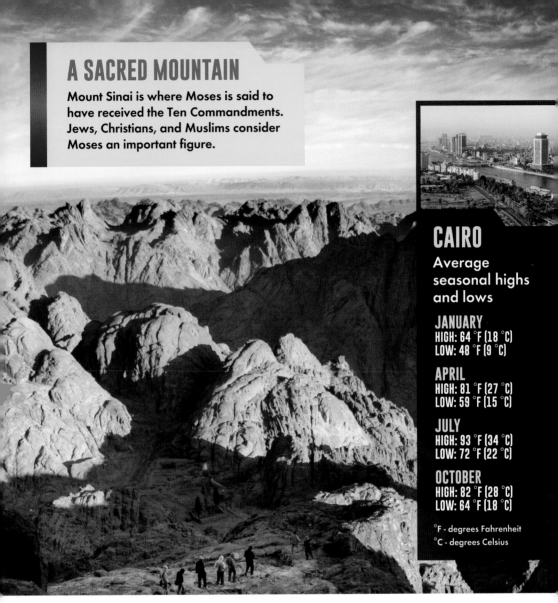

A SACRED MOUNTAIN

Mount Sinai is where Moses is said to have received the Ten Commandments. Jews, Christians, and Muslims consider Moses an important figure.

CAIRO

Average seasonal highs and lows

JANUARY
HIGH: 64 °F (18 °C)
LOW: 48 °F (9 °C)

APRIL
HIGH: 81 °F (27 °C)
LOW: 59 °F (15 °C)

JULY
HIGH: 93 °F (34 °C)
LOW: 72 °F (22 °C)

OCTOBER
HIGH: 82 °F (28 °C)
LOW: 64 °F (18 °C)

°F - degrees Fahrenheit
°C - degrees Celsius

Egyptian summers are hot and humid in the north. Temperatures can reach up to 123 degrees Fahrenheit (51 degrees Celsius). Winters are moderate with little rain. **Droughts** are common across the deserts. In spring, the *khamsin* wind blows from the Sahara. It is a hot, dusty wind that produces sandstorms.

Many kinds of wildlife call Egypt's harsh desert landscape home. Snakes, like the poisonous Egyptian cobra, slither in the sand. Desert monitors search for nests full of eggs while scorpions hide under rocks. Small groups of bearded aoudads and Dorcas gazelles graze on shrubs in the South Sahara. Birds of prey like kestrels and golden eagles cast shadows over the desert sand.

The **fertile** land around the Nile is also filled with life. Nile crocodiles grow as long as 20 feet (6 meters) in southern Egypt. Wading birds like egrets fish in the river alongside giant Nile perch.

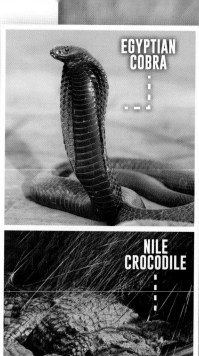

EGYPTIAN COBRA

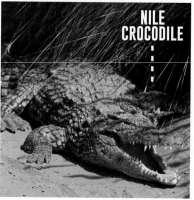

NILE CROCODILE

GREAT WHITE EGRET

CAMEL COUSINS

Egyptian camels are a type of camel called dromedaries. Unlike other camels, they have one hump instead of two!

AOUDAD

AOUDAD

Life Span: up to 10 years
Red List Status: vulnerable

aoudad range =

| LEAST CONCERN | NEAR THREATENED | VULNERABLE | ENDANGERED | CRITICALLY ENDANGERED | EXTINCT IN THE WILD | EXTINCT |

Egypt's largest population group is Egyptian Arab. They are **descendants** of Ancient Egyptians and the groups that invaded the land. Other groups traveled north from Sudan, and some continue to farm in the mountains. The Bedouin people are **nomads** who herd livestock like sheep or camels through the northern desert.

Most of Egypt's 97 million people are Sunni Muslims. Many others practice Egyptian Christianity. It dates back to the first century. Most people speak Egypt's national language of Egyptian Arabic as well as their own tribal languages.

FAMOUS FACE

Name: Mohamed Salah
Birthday: June 15, 1992
Hometown: Nagrig, Egypt
Famous for: A soccer forward who scored the 2 goals in a 2–1 win that qualified Egypt's national team for the 2018 World Cup

SPEAK ARABIC

Arabic uses script instead of letters. However, Arabic words can be written with the English alphabet so you can read them.

CAIRO

ENGLISH	ARABIC	HOW TO SAY IT
hello	marhaban	mar-HAB-ah
goodbye	ma'a as-salama	ma ahs-sah-LAH-mah
please (to males)	min fadlak	min FAHD-lehck
please (to females)	min fadlik	min FAHD-lick
thank you	shukran	SHUH-krahn
yes	na'am	NAHM
no	laa	LAH-ah

CAIRO

Over one-third of all Egyptians live in **urban** areas. Cities like Cairo or Alexandria are crowded and noisy. Scooters, cars, buses, and taxis fill the streets. Boats called feluccas sail on the Nile. Most people live in apartment buildings made of concrete or brick.

In **rural** villages, families live in small houses of just one or two rooms. They are made of mud brick and sometimes painted in bright colors. Houses are built close together to keep land open for farming. Most people in rural areas move from place to place using donkeys or camels.

TRADITIONAL STYLE

Traditional Muslim clothing is not required in Egypt, but many women still wear the hijab head covering. Some still wear long robes called *abayas*.

Many Egyptians are fun-loving and enjoy spending time with friends and family. During greetings, men exchange handshakes and a kiss on each cheek. Women do the same. Men and women greet each other verbally unless the women offer to shake hands first. Egyptians take pride in their homes and like to have friends over to share a meal. Visitors remove shoes before entering the house and quietly leave a small gift behind for the hostess.

Egyptians often have big families. Children are considered blessings. Extended family usually lives nearby. Cousins, aunts, uncles, and grandparents may get together for weekends and holidays.

AN ANCIENT LANGUAGE

Ancient Egyptians had their own way of writing called hieroglyphs. It was a combination of symbols and pictures. There were over 700 hieroglyphs in the Egyptian alphabet!

Children receive six years of elementary school beginning at age 6 followed by three years of preparatory school. Then, students may choose to attend secondary school for three years. They can train for a trade or technical job or prepare for university. Egypt has many universities in Cairo and Alexandria.

Many city workers have **service jobs** like retail, government services, and **tourism**. Farmers in the Nile Valley grow fruit, vegetables, and cotton. Factory workers turn the cotton into cloth. Miners and oil workers dig for resources. Egypt exports fruit and vegetables, **textiles**, and oil products.

RESTAURANT WORKER

FARMER

19

SOCCER

Soccer is Egypt's national sport. People cheer for the national team and for their favorite clubs. Children play soccer for hours. They also play volleyball and basketball. Wrestling and weightlifting are favorite sports as well.

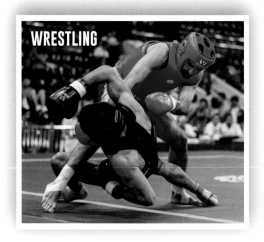

WRESTLING

Many people enjoy sailing on the Mediterranean Sea or the Nile River. Watching TV and listening to music are popular pastimes. Most of all, Egyptians like to spend time with friends. Men go to coffee houses where they talk over the day's news. Women often meet with their friends at each other's homes or chat at the market.

SAILING

THE BLIND CAT GAME

What You Need:
- at least five players
- 1 blindfold

Instructions:

1. Choose an area to play and set the boundaries. Boundaries can be a grassy yard, half a tennis court, or an area of playground. Set backpacks or chalk lines to signify borders.

2. Choose the first player to be the cat. They will wear the blindfold.

3. The blind cat tries to tag one of the other players. The other players cannot go outside of the boundaries. Make it hard! Creep around and meow to confuse the blind cat!

4. The first player to be tagged will be the next blind cat.

FINGER FOOD

Egyptian teens love fast food as much as Americans do. *Shawarma* sandwiches and *falafel* are delicious street foods. Burgers, pizza, and Chinese takeout are available in Cairo.

Beans and bread are part of almost every Egyptian meal. Breakfast might be a bowl of *ful medames*, which is similar to fava bean porridge. Egypt's national dish is *koshari*. It is a common lunchtime meal that includes lentils, rice, and a spicy tomato chile sauce. Dinners often include vegetable stews or leftovers from lunch.

Fresh fruit or rice pudding are favorite desserts. Many people eat a late snack, too. Ful dip with vegetables is a common choice. Grape leaves stuffed with rice is another favorite.

KOSHARI

FUL MEDAMES

Ingredients
1 16-ounce can fava beans or pinto beans, undrained

2 tablespoons lemon juice

2 tablespoons olive oil

1 teaspoon garlic powder

salt and pepper to taste

fresh parsley for garnish

Steps
1. With the help of an adult, put beans and their liquid into a small pot on the stove. Bring to a boil over medium heat.

2. When it reaches a boil, reduce the heat and simmer for five minutes.

3. Pour the beans into a large bowl. Mash the beans into a paste with a fork or a potato masher.

4. Add the rest of the ingredients and mix well.

5. Sprinkle the chopped parsley on top. Serve with pita bread.

EID AL-FITR

January begins with joyful New Year's Day and Egyptian Christmas celebrations. In April or May, *Sham al-Nessim* celebrates spring with picnics and outdoor activities. The holy month of Ramadan is celebrated each year. Muslims **fast** from sunup to sundown. Then, Ramadan ends with a three-day festival called *Eid al-Fitr*.

On July 23, Egypt celebrates its Revolution Day with parades and music. A popular **tradition** during *Mawlid al-Nabi* is mawlid candies. Mawlid candies are large dolls and horses molded from sugar and decorated in colored paper. Egypt takes pride in its ancient traditions!

MAWLID AL-NABI

AROUND 2630 BCE
The first pyramid, "Step Pyramid," is built at Saqqara for pharaoh Djoser of the Third Dynasty

647 CE
After years of invasion, the entire country of Egypt is under Islamic rule

1869
Suez Canal opens, connecting the Mediterranean and Red Seas

1882
The British start to colonize Egypt

1936
At age 16, King Farouk becomes king

1952
Revolution turns
Egypt into a republic

1973
Egypt and Syria begin
fighting Israel in the
Yom Kippur War

1967
Israel attacks Egypt in the
Six-Day War in response to
Egypt blocking the shipping
route in the Gulf of Aqaba

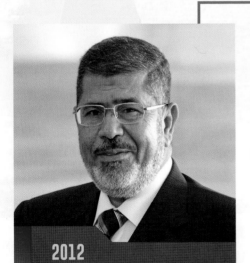

2014
Egyptian voters approve
a new constitution

2012
Egypt holds its first free
presidential election and
elects Mohamed Morsi

27

EGYPT FACTS

Official Name: Arab Republic of Egypt

Flag of Egypt: Three equal horizontal stripes of red, white, and black. Black represents the oppression the people have suffered. Red stands for the bloody struggle to overcome the oppression. White is shown for the nation's bright future. In the middle is the national emblem: a gold eagle with a shield over its chest sitting above a scroll with Egypt written in Arabic.

Area: 386,662 square miles
(1,001,450 square kilometers)

Capital City: Cairo

Important Cities: Alexandria, Port Said, Luxor

Population:
97,041,072 (July 2017)

WHERE PEOPLE LIVE

COUNTRYSIDE
56.7%

CITY
43.3%

MANUFACTURING
23.5%

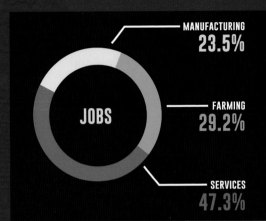

JOBS

FARMING
29.2%

SERVICES
47.3%

Main Exports:

oil products

cotton

chemicals

textiles

fruits and
vegetables

metal
products

National Holiday:
Revolution Day (July 23)

Main Language:
Arabic

Form of Government:
presidential republic

Title for Country Leaders:
president and prime minister

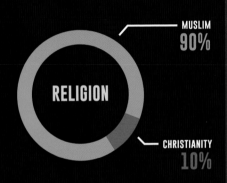

RELIGION

MUSLIM
90%

CHRISTIANITY
10%

Unit of Money:
Egyptian pound

GLOSSARY

Arab—related to people who are originally from the Arabian Peninsula and who now live mostly in the Middle East and northern Africa

arid—not having enough rainfall to support farming

canal—a waterway for boats

descendants—people related to a person or group of people who lived at an earlier time

droughts—long periods of dry weather

fast—to stop eating all foods or particular foods for a time

fertile—able to support growth

gulf—part of an ocean or sea that extends into land

nomads—people who have no fixed home but wander from place to place

oasis—a green spot in a desert that can support farming

peninsula—a section of land that extends out from a larger piece of land and is almost completely surrounded by water

pharaoh—a ruler of ancient Egypt

rural—related to the countryside

service jobs—jobs that perform tasks for people or businesses

textiles—woven or knit cloth

tourism—the business of people traveling to visit other places

tradition—a custom, idea, or belief handed down from one generation to the next

urban—related to cities and city life

TO LEARN MORE

AT THE LIBRARY

Hart, George. *Ancient Egypt*. New York, N.Y.: DK Publishing, 2014.

Pateman, Robert, Salwa El-Hamamsy and Josie Elias. *Egypt*. New York, N.Y.: Cavendish Square Publishing, 2015.

Stanborough, Rebecca. *The Great Pyramid of Giza*. North Mankato, Minn.: Capstone Press, 2016.

ON THE WEB

Learning more about Egypt is as easy as 1, 2, 3.

1. Go to www.factsurfer.com.

2. Enter "Egypt" into the search box.

3. Click the "Surf" button and you will see a list of related web sites.

With factsurfer.com, finding more information is just a click away.

INDEX

The images in this book are reproduced through the courtesy of: rayints, front cover; javarman, pp. 4-5; Graficam Ahmed Saeed, p. 5 (top); suronin, p. 5 (middle top); Radovan1, p. 5 (middle bottom); Anton Belo, p. 5 (bottom); Anton_Ivanov, p. 8; Maxim Tarasyugin, p. 9 (top); Orhan Cam p. 9 (bottom); Alberto Loyo, p. 10 (top); davemhuntphotography, p. 10 (middle top); alredosaz, p. 10 (middle bottom); Eric Isselee, p. 10 (bottom); GizmoPhoto, p. 11; night_cat, p. 12; Marco Iacobucci EPP, p. 13 (top); Egyptian Studio, p. 13 (bottom); eFesenko, pp. 14, 15; Emad Omar Farouk, p. 16; Andrew McConnell/ Alamy, p. 17; Claudia Wiens/ Alamy, p. 18; Buhairi Nawawi, p. 19 (top); frans lemmens/ Alamy, p. 19 (bottom); Islam Safwat/ Alamy, p. 20 (top); Chen WS, p. 20 (bottom); Patryk Kosmider, p. 21 (top); Iakov Filimonov, p. 21 (bottom); Megapress/ Alamy, p. 22; Fanfo, p. 23 (top)(bottom); Zuma Press, Inc./ Alamy, p. 24; AFP/Stringer/ Getty, p. 25; Murat Hajdarhodzic, p. 26 (top); Thutmoselll/ Wikipedia, p. 26 (bottom); Agência Brasil/ Wikipedia, p. 27; Nick Fielding/ Alamy, p. 29 (left); Fat Jackey, p. 29 (right).